WASIM ONE-STAR

For Lettie, in loving memory

WASIM
ONE - STAR

Chris Ashley

F

FRANCES LINCOLN
CHILDREN'S BOOKS

Chapter One

Wasim had to be first.

"Oy, Wasim! Wasim! Miss, he's knocked my graph off the wall."

Wasim, first at the door and staring like a guardsman at 110 cm on the height chart, spun round as fast as his bulging United rucksack would let him.

"Tell him, Miss."

Wasim had to be first whenever there was a line, but today was special. Today was swimming day – the last swimming day.

Today Wasim really had to be first and somebody, Ben Perry it sounded like, was trying to ruin it by getting him done. Wasim would get sent to the back and time would be wasted. The last swimming day, free time for most groups and for Wasim's group, the splash group, the chance to do their One Star. From the steps at the deep end to the steps

at the shallow end, twenty-five metres. And then on Friday there'd be Mr Abbott in the sharing assembly, doing his television voice while he gave out the certificate. "Wasim Ahmed," he'd say. "You're a star."

A One Star, that was what it was, a big red star on your certificate.

Twenty-five metres – gulping, spluttering, no armbands – a red star on a piece of card. One Star.

There was a sharp dig in Wasim's back. Ben was trying once again.

"Miss?"

"Oh, just be sensible for one minute," Mrs Scott snapped.

Wasim couldn't believe his luck and he turned back to the height chart. Miss was still busy with the dinner money.

"But, Miss, he's pushed in and knocked –"

"Ben, I am busy!"

Wasim stared even harder at the height chart and waited until his senses told him that Mrs Scott had turned back to the pile of Monday money on her desk. Then he allowed himself the flare of his nostrils and the "Sss… sss… sss," that would send Ben barmy.

"Miss! He's laughing, Miss.

Just because –"

Mrs Scott finally bashed the Tuppaware container they all called the money tin on to the table.

"OK, Ben," she was saying in a whisper that sounded louder than one of Mr Abbott's shouts. "Since you have such a problem with Wasim you had better go and be Neil's partner. Go on."

Wasim gave a secret flare of his nostrils. Neil was nowhere near the front. A scowling Ben began pushing his way back.

"And er, Wayne, you go up with Wasim."

Mrs Scott paused and then said it more carefully.

"Wayne, you go with Wasim."

But Wasim was going to sort it out.

Wayne Ho was new. He was new to the school and new to the country. He didn't speak much English yet and Wasim knew what it was like when you had different words for things at home.

He knew what it was like when the only school word you knew was Miss. What you needed was someone like

him, Wasim, to help you out. He barged back down the line, accidentally brushing two graphs on to the floor with his rucksack, and pulled Wayne up to the front.

"Oy, Wasim!"

"Ahmed!"

But they were only breathing it now because Miss was looking down at the money and they were late already.

Wasim stood at attention again and waited. He nudged Wayne until the new boy stood at attention too. Then he stared again at 110 cm and thought about his One Star. Twenty-five metres and no armbands!

Chapter Two

Finally, Junior S got away.

Mrs Scott had seen the graphs and looked at Wasim, her eyes never leaving his while she bent down, picked them up and put them silently on to the bookshelf next to the display.

"Don't worry, I'll pick them up," she said. Which meant that somebody else should have.

"Miss, it wasn't –"

But Mrs Scott didn't say any more

and that told Wasim to stop.

He'd have to show that he was a particularly good leader on the walk, though. Especially when it came to not following Miss into the road. Nicola Harris had forgotten last week and not waited for the signal to follow.

"Stop there! How many times ...?"

Mrs Scott had shouted. She didn't shout often, but she did when it came to roads. Even at Nicola Harris.

Wasim led them in silence down past the assembly and allowed himself a glance through the hall door at the piano where the certificates would be piled.

Then he walked importantly on. He smiled at Wayne. Things were going well.

He did his special walk under the subway. It was fast but you didn't run, and at each kerb he put a hand out to stop Wayne and sensibly waited for Mrs Scott, who seemed a bit out of breath.

"Wayne's not your real name, is it?" Samantha Waterworth shouted from behind. "Doesn't sound right with Ho, and when you're Chinese or Japanese ..."

16

"Hong Kong he comes from, don't you, Wayne?" Gemma came right up beside them. "Miss said so."

Wasim pushed her back into her place. It was his job to talk to Wayne.

"Shut up, Waterworth," he said.

"You shut up, Wasim. Miss!"

But Mrs Scott was still puffing to keep up with Wasim's special walk and she pretended not to hear. Wasim quickly got chatting before she changed her mind.

"Are you in our group – splash group?"

Wayne just smiled, friendly. He didn't say a lot.

Wasim tried it in his own home words, Urdu, whispering in case Gemma took the mickey out of it.

But Wayne just smiled again.

"D'you have armbands? You'll be with us."

Wayne looked puzzled, so Wasim mimed armbands and followed Mrs Scott into the road.

"Wasim Ahmed!"

Wasim jumped and scuttled back to Wayne on the pavement, saying, "So?" before Gemma had a chance to say anything. He pushed his glasses up and finally allowed himself to meet Mrs Scott's glare.

"Do not step off the pavement until I signal. Is that clear?"

"Miss!"

Of course it was clear, he was the best in the class at knowing that. "So?" he hissed at no one in particular.

Wasim felt somebody laughing behind him, but Mrs Scott was still looking at him and they were crossing the road now which meant he couldn't do anything anyway. So for the last few streets Wasim just thought about the steps, the steps up at the deep end. The rough plastic on the soles of his feet, the slow cool that would spread up his legs as he went down and then make his chest stop thumping as it spread over his tummy.

Then there would be the terrible moment when John the swimming teacher made him let go. He'd feel nothingness under his feet and then the cool would become cold and move up to his throat and his mouth would start gasping and his legs would start

wriggling and ... and that was all he
knew. Last time that had been all there
was to it. Wasim had stopped going
down and suddenly felt as if he was
flying. Well he was in a way, he was
floating. He'd had armbands on but
straight away Andrew
Foster had jumped in
behind him and told
him to shove up.
So he'd wriggled

20

and gulped and spluttered up to the shallow end. "Miss!" he'd shouted when he got there. And Mrs Scott had put her hands above her head and clapped. That was last time!

A warm smell of feet hit Wasim and he put a hand out to stop Wayne. That was the swimming smell.

One more corner. Now Wasim's stomach started turning again. What if he didn't float? What if his legs didn't start kicking and he didn't start reaching and pulling like John and Dad kept telling him? What if he didn't do it and had to grab the pole before he got to the shallow steps?

"Oy, Wasim, move it. What you stopped for?" and there was a push as the line came to a spluttering halt and Wayne was bundled into him. What if he didn't do it?

"Ahmed!" came another shout.

Wasim began to walk again and found that his mouth was too dry even to tell Gemma to shut up. He'd do it… wouldn't he? Twenty-five metres. No armbands.

Chapter Three

The big glass doors opened and
the smell of feet, Dettol and
chloreysomething filled Wasim's head
and got mixed up with shouts half
echoed and then lost in distant
splashes. Blue glittered and danced on
the ceiling, teasing the children about
what they would see behind the big
window as soon as Mrs Scott had
finished signing them in. Wasim had
to put his hands in his pockets to stop

himself from pushing her, but finally they were in.

"First look!" Wasim had spun round to say it and there it was, the pool – blue and beautiful and long, very long. One Star long.

"Second!" said Samantha.

"First worst!" shouted Gemma. But it wasn't being nasty, they were all too happy.

Wasim wanted to be first into the Boys, to get the best peg next to the warm door, but Wayne had walked on and was following Gemma and Samantha. Some of the boys, crushing through their door, started laughing.

"Wayne's going into the Girls!" they cried and tried those whistles where you put your fingers into your mouth.

Wasim would miss the warm peg.
He thought for a second but then he
elbowed his way out.

Wayne needed him, he remembered,
and being first wouldn't matter today,
not One Star day. He rushed up the
corridor.

"Wayne, Wayne!" The shouts
bounced off the tiles and the
hot chocolate machine.

"Do not shout in my pool!"

Everyone froze. It was Carol, the other swimming teacher, the younger one, coming out of her room. The girls all said they liked her – but that was just because she looked like Lara Croft. She just screamed at everyone all the time and Wasim was really glad that she didn't take the splash group.

She glared down at Wasim.

"Do you behave like that all the time? I'd hate to live in your house."

Carol made it sound as if living in Wasim's house would be the worst thing in the world and he wasn't sure that it was just because of his shouting.

"Problem?" Mrs Scott was there and Wasim felt safe again, just like he always did in school.

"Miss, M …" Wasim couldn't explain

quickly enough.

"Miss, Wayne was going into the Girls," Nicola said.

"Oh, he's never been to the baths before. Come on, Wayne."

Carol glared at Wasim and he could tell she was cross that Miss hadn't joined in telling him off. She banged through the swing door and the splashes and shouts that came through from the pool hit Wasim like a great wave.

"Miss, what group is Wayne in?" Gemma asked, still giggling.

"Non-swimmers," replied Mrs Scott. "We've sorted this all out with Mum, haven't we, Wayne?"

Wayne smiled.

"Wayne's in the non-swimmers."

"But what if he can swim his Three Star or the Bronze or something, Miss?"

"It doesn't matter if you can swim to the moon. Until I see you swim, you're a non-swimmer and you stay in the shallow end."

The girls giggled going through their red door and Mrs Scott turned to Wasim.

"Stay with him, Wasim. Splash group, is that clear?"

"Miss."

Wasim felt tall and excited again now. He put an arm around Wayne to lead him into the Boys and gave him a thumbs up. Wayne gave one back. That seemed to work.

Wasim wouldn't have got the best peg anyway. A group from the

High School were in and all the boys from Wasim's class were getting changed in silence, just listening to the big ones and keeping out of their way. The older ones had hold of one kid's trunks and were throwing them around.

Wasim nodded at a peg and he and Wayne got changed quickly, ducking whenever the wet trunks were thrown near them.

"Quick as you can, lads." John came in from the pool. The High School kids pretended to get dressed sensibly and the boy who owned the trunks went and picked them up as if it were his fault they were on the floor. The swimming teacher must have known something was going on because he stayed, arms folded, foot tapping.

The relieved Junior S boys got changed at double speed and skidded under his towering figure. Then it was up the steps, through the footbath and the freezing showers, and on to the poolside.

Wasim was third ready. Not bad considering. But he waited for Wayne. He showed his new friend how to dodge the shower spray and then he too was on the poolside.

He blanked out the noises and splashes, and shivered. It was not just that a few drops of the shower had hit him, it was also because he was looking at the two sets of steps. He'd seen them a hundred times before but never like today. Never when they meant so much. Never when he would have to grab that round, glittering steel, watch his face turn into funny shapes on its shiny surface and then let himself drop into the blue. Never when getting between the steps up near the Girls and the steps at the shallow end meant everything. "*Wasim Ahmed … You're a star.*" That would be Friday. Wasim hugged himself.

He'd do it, he'd do it. And then the whistle blew.

"Right, Splash group, yes? You've got me today. John's with the High School."

Oh no, Wasim thought. Not Carol. Not Carol for his One Star.

Chapter Four

"Do not run!"

There were nine of them left once the Two Star, Three Star and Bronze groups had walked off with their floats for free time. The nine were non-swimmers ... until today. By the end of today, some of them – most of them – would be One Stars... swimmers.

Wayne had begun to follow the others but Mrs Scott, in her pumps, had been walking round ready to look after her group up at the deep end.

"No, Wayne. You stay here in the shallow end until we can see what you can do." She pointed to where Wasim was standing and Wayne, who did everything that he understood first time, came and stood with Wasim.

There was a huge cheer from the deep end as the other groups dived, jumped and bombed into the water. The Splash group grinned at each other. They'd be in any second now. Wasim could almost taste the water as he imagined his special jump and spit-out. Then, once they were used to the water, they'd go up for the twenty-five metre swim.

Wasim gave Wayne another thumbs up and waited. Come on. Come on.

Carol was talking and they hadn't been told to get in yet. She was with one of the lifeguards in his bright yellow polo shirt and shorter than short shorts. He was leaning against the wall and she was laughing. Come on … come on.

At last the lifeguard went back to his special seat at the 1.5 metre mark. The Splash group looked at each other again and some hopeful smiles broke out.

But then the yellow shirt turned and said something about a rota which Carol didn't seem to like. She put her hands on her hips and started talking again. Nine pairs of eyes pleaded with each other and Andrew looked up at the clock and flashed his hands twice.

"Twenty minutes," he mouthed.

Then Gemma spoke up. Good old Gemma, thought Wasim. She wasn't so bad.

"Miss? When are we going in?"

Carol turned and looked as if someone had stabbed her with a spear or something.

"When … I … am … good … and … ready."

But Gemma would probably look like Lara Croft herself one day and Carol usually liked her. Carol raised her eyes to the heavens and then looked at the Splash group as if she was doing them a big favour.

"It's free time, isn't it? Go and choose yourselves a float each," she said and turned back to Yellow Shirt.

Donna and Jamila nudged each other and skipped off. Nobody else moved. The One Star. Who was going to say something about the One Star? Gemma wasn't, she was already shaking her head. Wasim took a deep breath ... but then he let it out. Why should it be him? But the others had seen it and knew there was a chance of him doing it. Andrew was nudging him and Gemma had her hands on her hips and her eyebrows raised.

Wasim gulped in another breath.

"Miss ... Miss ... Miss ..." It still happened when he was excited. "Miss" was all that would come out.

"You are going to get on my nerves, young man. Choose your floats. Are you disobeying me?"

"Miss … M …"

Carol turned purple, but Wasim was going to get it out. "Miss … we've got to do our One Star, Miss."

There was silence. Even the shrieks from the kids in the water seemed to stop. The lifeguard gave Carol a look and walked off to his chair. But he didn't sit in it. He looked back to see what Carol would do.

"And who says?"

That was it. They all knew it then. Carol wasn't going to let them do it!

"John said, Miss." It was Gemma and they all looked at her. Wasim decided he was going to give her his prawn cocktail crisps after. "John said last week, Miss."

Nothing happened. Gemma knew

what she was doing. John was in charge, he ran the pool. They all knew he was above Carol. Nothing happened. Donna and Jamila climbed in and started jumping up and down keeping their heads out of the water. The rest of them waited.

Wayne looked puzzled.

"Do not move."

They weren't going to. Carol gave them a last glare and, with her arms folded to show she was taking her time, she walked in slow motion to where John was crouching next to the group of High School children. The Splash group watched as John looked up. No one breathed. Carol's arm flapped in their direction and, shivering again, Wasim tried to swallow.

John was looking at them
and ... John was nodding.
Yes, yes, yes! John was nodding.

Carol, her arms still folded, began
a long, slow walk back while they all
looked at the floor in case she saw
them being pleased. Wasim, though,
looked up through his eyebrows and
managed to meet Andrew's eyes.

He flared his nostrils wide and he could see Andrew killing himself not to laugh. Wasim hoped he wouldn't, as that really would ruin it.

Carol got back to them and snatched a pole from the wall. They were going. "Not a sound," was all she said and she led the way up towards the steps while Wasim looked at every tile on the bottom and tried to imagine every droplet of water as he began the twenty-five metre walk that in a few seconds he would be trying to swim.

He'd let somebody else be first, he decided, just for once. Somebody overtook. Let them, thought Wasim. It was Wayne, his straight cropped hair bouncing as he walked.

No, Wayne wouldn't be doing his

One Star, would he? He hadn't even done his width for Miss yet. No, no, he should be down there with Donna and Jamila.

Wasim tapped Wayne's back. Wayne turned and smiled. Wasim thrust his thumb back in the direction of the shallow end. Wayne kept walking.

"Back!" said Wasim, but it was too quiet. "Back!" he hissed. But this time it was too loud. He knew before it had finished coming out that it was too loud and yes, Carol had stopped.

"Right. I don't even need to ask who that was, do I? I said silence and I am already more than fed up with you."

"M … Miss …"

But she had turned, dangerously slowly, and was almost at the steps now. Wasim had to tell Wayne without talking. Wasim tapped him. Wayne ignored it. He knew what getting in trouble meant and Carol's mood was Carol's mood in every language in the world. So Wasim did it.

He grabbed Wayne's shoulders, turned him round and tried to push him back to the shallow end. Wayne, looking hurt, broke free and turned back. Wasim tried again. He reached out, got Wayne's shoulders and… it was then that Carol turned round.

All the smells, all the sounds, all the colours and

Wayne's hurt, puzzled face, they all crowded in on Wasim and got jumbled up. Only one thing was clear. It was one of Carol's words in between all the stuff she was shouting about Wasim fighting in the line. It echoed through his head and it made him feel sick. It was, "Out!" She'd said, "Out!" and she was pointing at the changing room. "Out!" The pool was silent now. "Out. You'll have to do it next week."

Wasim tried to breathe. There wasn't a next week, it was the holidays. This was it until his class's turn next year.

Wasim found that he had carried

on walking. He was the only person moving in the whole pool. He was right up with her now. He'd explain. "Miss, M …" He needed time for the right words. "Miss."

But Carol wasn't going to give him any time. "Out! Out!"

So that was it. Wasim turned, a huge sob was coming up and he had to get out before it exploded out of his mouth and down his nose. He turned and

walked with his elbows pumping,
glaring at the ground, then at them all,
at Wayne and at Gemma.

"So?" he managed to spit at Donna
looking up at him from the shallow
end. And then he'd finished his walk
and he was past the steps.

Twenty-five metres. No
armbands and no One Star.

Chapter Five

Wasim did what he always did first and put on his glasses. But he was crying now, sitting on the bench under his peg really sobbing, and so his glasses just steamed up… useless. A huge rolling tickle went through him and he wanted to hit something or throw something or scream out loud. Then he thought of tonight, going in through his front door and not being able to tell them that he'd done it, passed.

He wanted home now, Mum and Dad, Shamaila his little sister and Atif his brother. He thought about his house and all the love that was in it. His house and how Carol had said she'd hate to live there. Well, he'd hate to have her there... How dare she say that. He'd never let her in his house and he knew why she'd really hate to live there. Well, he couldn't be sure but...

Wasim took his glasses off and wiped them while he thought of his dad taking time off to practise swimming on the last two Saturdays. He was cold. He pulled his towel from his rucksack and a piece of paper fell out. Wasim wiped his glasses again and picked it out of the puddle. His glasses were still no good so he squinted and read it without them.

"Good luck."

Wasim heaved again in a great gulp.

"What's that say, then? That's not English."

Wasim jumped, startled.

"What's it say?" The kid was coming over. He was from the High School, the small one whose trunks the others had thrown around.

"Nothing." Wasim stuffed the note back into his bag.

"Please yourself. What's up with you, then?"

Wasim pulled his bag down and began searching for his shirt. He could remember stuffing it down there somewhere.

"You the one that got chucked out?"

"So?" Wasim searched harder to stop the tears coming again.

"They nicked my trunks so I can't go in, can I. We were doing our lifesavers. We, we ..." The boy was cuffing his nose.

Wasim stopped punching in his bag and looked up. The boy said a swear word and brushed an arm across his eyes. Wasim felt sorry for him.

"It said 'Good luck', my note."

"Oh," said the boy.

Wasim forgot about his shirt and started pulling on his trousers which he'd found under the bench. He looked up.

"Do you want these?" His trunks were still dry.

The boy sniffed again, "No, you're all right. They'll all be out in a minute."

Wasim pulled his trousers up over his trunks and sat down again.

"Here …" The boy was up again. "Have a laugh. Don't tell no one, eh?" The boy had gone over to a big metal door, the warm door where Wasim liked to get a peg. "We always go in here when no one's around. Come on."

The door was opened and Wasim was hit by a great balloon of heat. "Come on, it's a grin."

Wasim didn't move.

"Come on. What are they going to do, chuck you out?" The boy disappeared and Wasim got up. Then he sat down.

The boy's head popped back. "Come on."

This would mean trouble. Wasim looked at the steps leading up to the poolside and heard the shouts of everyone having fun. And then he heard some clapping. He knew what that was for. Yeah, what could they do, chuck him out? This would mean real trouble, but somehow he was heading towards the darkness and the heat.

"Shut the door."

Wasim couldn't see anything. He could just feel the warmth and hear a great humming noise.

"It's the boiler. It heats up the water."

Things were getting clearer and Wasim could make out a blue light where the voice was coming from.

"Come on over here, quick."

Wasim put his hands out like a tightrope walker and edged past the shadowy heat of three huge shuddering machines.

"This is it. Look. Like portholes. That's the pool."

Wasim reached the boy and the blue light. Yes, they were portholes, two of them, like windows on a ship, and that was the pool. He was looking through a window into the deep end. Underwater.

"Look at his mug!" The boy laughed and suddenly Wasim was laughing too. He was roaring. Through the window he could see Ben Perry trying to get something, a brick, off the bottom of the pool. But what a face he was pulling and yuk, there was stuff coming out of his nose! Wait till Wasim got back to school and told everybody that. He'd tell them when they were all eating, that'd show Ben up. Wasim laughed again and looked through the other porthole. Someone's legs were

coming down the steps right next to
the window. The legs started moving
and Wasim lost sight of them in the
thick blue glass. That would be
someone doing their One Star.

Wasim's smile died, but the boy was
pulling him back to the top window
and Wasim could see why. Here was
Ben again, going for the brick and this
time his trunks were coming off and

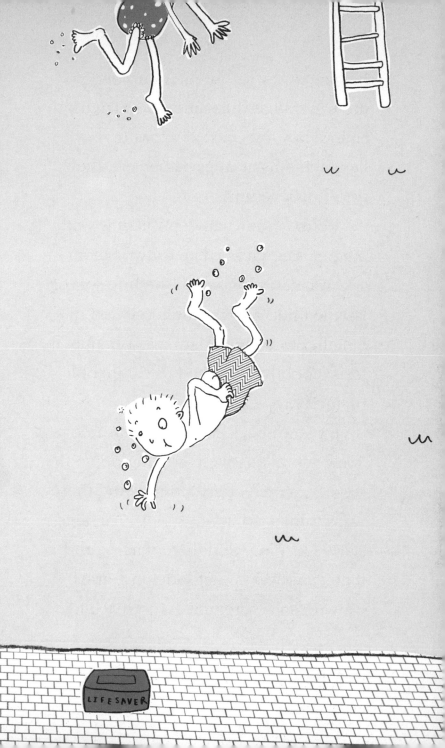

he was trying to pull them up and get the brick all at the same time. The High School boy was curled up with laughter. Wasim hugged himself, they'd never believe this.

"What's your name?" Wasim would have to know for when he told them.

"Titch, Titch Jarvis." The boy sort of laughed but Wasim didn't know whether to or not. Maybe it was only in his school that you had to call people by their proper names.

He went back to the other window. Some more legs were coming down the steps … slowly, very slowly. And there were trunks, so it was a boy. The legs started kicking, and there was … and there was Wayne, legs kicking, arms clawing, face screaming and reaching,

silently
reaching up
to the air and
sinking past
Wasim's glass.
But Wasim had gone.

He sped through the
darkness, letting the burns
from the huge machines
on his bare sides guide him
back to the chinks of light
where the door was. He crashed it
open, ran through the changing room,
made a mini-tidal wave in the foot-bath
and slipped on the steps. He hardly
had a breath left but he pulled himself
up by the hand rail and finally reached
the poolside.

Which way? He headed for the

steps – he'd know where they were in his sleep – and banged straight into a hard body. It was John, herding his group back to the changing rooms.

"What …?"

"Miss, Mm …" Wasim knew nothing would come out, so he dragged John's shirt and turned

him to face the steps at the deep end where Carol, her back to the water, was chatting to her lifeguard friend.

John looked down at him. Wasim pointed again and this time John was off, moving like a bullet along the side and into the water without a splash.

There was a second, a silent second, two, three, and then there was a huge bubble and one…

two heads came out of the water.
Still there was silence and then a wail,
a huge wail from Wayne.

Wasim realised that he had been
holding his own breath too. He took in
a great lungful of air and let out a wail
of his own.

Chapter Six

He wasn't very good at looking as if he didn't care. Wasim cared about everything he did. Sometimes that led to praise for hard work, like with his reading, and sometimes it led to arguments, like when he was playing football in the playground or when he moaned at somebody on his table for losing a group point. And now, in Friday assembly with his mum sitting at the back with all the other mums and

dads, it meant that he couldn't sit still
and laugh and clap with the others
when Mr Abbott handed over a white
certificate and said, "Andrew Foster,
you are a star."

It wasn't very funny really anyway.

What was worse was that he could
feel as many eyes on him
as on the lucky things out
at the front. Everyone
knew what had

happened on Monday. They'd talked about it all week and up until today it had felt good. But today there was no getting away from it – whatever else he had done, he had not swum that twenty-five metres from the deep steps to the shallow steps.

Nicola was next up and Wasim slowly forced himself to clap. Then he saw Miss looking and clapped a bit faster.

He looked round for Donna and Jamila. They were the only other two who hadn't got a certificate. They were clapping like anything and Wasim forced his hands together again while he sneaked a look at the clock. Topic time next, then break.

"And now, boys and girls, we've got one more star."

Wasim jerked up. Donna hadn't done it, had she?

But Mr Abbott wasn't talking about swimming; he was talking about something else, rules again. Wasim began cleaning the crack between two floor tiles while Mr Abbott went on about something to do with the school rule about calling people by their own names. Something about a boy who

had come from another country and
who had been so worried that nobody
would say his name properly that
he had chosen a footballer's name,
a United player's name. There was a
buzz and Wasim stopped picking at
the crack. "Just," Mr Abbott whispered
in his very quietest specially-for-infants
voice, "to make it easy for people
to say."

Heads twizzled everywhere. Who
was it? Mr Abbott waited until they
settled down.

"But," he told them finally, "the boy
had found a really good friend, a friend
who was willing to give up things, very
important things, like a special
certificate, to help him. And because
of this friend, the new boy trusted

everybody at the school to be just as kind. So from now on," Mr Abbott was walking down the middle and smiling, "we are all going to call Wayne by his proper name – Wing Ho."

They all swung round to where Junior S were sitting and everybody in the hall tried saying it … "Wing Ho."

It wasn't that hard and Wayne, Wing Ho, was beaming from ear to ear.

Then Mr Abbott called for quiet again and said, "I reckon a friend such as Wing Ho has found is a very special friend, don't you?"

They all said yes.

"Let's give him a big cheer then, shall we. Come up here, Wasim Ahmed. You really are a star."

All that had happened an hour before. The rest of his class were doing their Vikings work now but Wasim had a tight grip on the rail, his foot on the first rough plastic step, and he was staring down through the shimmering water to see how deep 1.5 metres actually was.

It was deep. What if he didn't make it? Mr Abbott had driven him and Wing Ho to the High School and then on to the baths in his Mondeo. He was missing a meeting just to give Wasim a chance of his One Star.

"OK, Wasim? Take your time." It was John with the pole. There was no sign of Carol but there was a new lady on the other side doing a lifesaving test with Peter Jarvis.

Wasim looked down again. What if he didn't make it? He gripped the rail harder, had one last look along the pool and there, right down there by the other steps was Wayne. No, not Wayne, Wing Ho, and Wing Ho was shouting and clapping.

So what if he didn't make it.
Wasim was already a star. He let go.
Twenty-five metres, he thought, and
no armbands.

Read about Wasim's football skills in
Wasim the Wanderer.

CHRIS ASHLEY

Chris Ashley is a headteacher and it was when
he took a class of children for their weekly swim
that an adventure just like Wasim's unfolded.

"I could see that one boy who couldn't swim
wasn't listening to the instructor and sure enough,
he jumped straight into the deep end. We fished him
out and it was almost a happy ending," recalls Chris,
"except that as I got out of the water I remembered
that I was wearing my best suit!"

Chris loves swimming and football and has also
written about Wasim's football skills in
Wasim the Wanderer.

Also available from
Frances Lincoln Children's Books

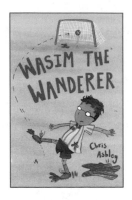

Wasim the Wanderer

Chris Ashley
Illustrated by Kate Pankhurst

No one at school can score a goal like Wasim!
So he is trying out his football skills for
Teamwork 10,000 and that might just lead to
a trial with the Woodley Wanderers! But how
can he play his best football with Robert Bailey
lurking around every corner – and then
on the football pitch too?

ISBN 978-1-84507-776-1

Dear Whiskers

Ann Whitehead Nagda
Illustrated by Stephanie Roth

Everyone in Jenny's class has to write a letter to
someone in another class. Only you have to pretend
to be a mouse! Jenny thinks the whole thing
is really silly… until her penfriend writes back.
There is something mysterious about Jenny's
penfriend. Will Jenny discover her secret?

ISBN: 978-1-84507-563-7

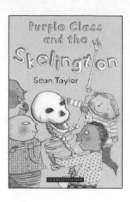

Purple Class and the Skelington

Sean Taylor
Illustrated by Helen Bate

Meet Purple Class – there is Jamal who often
forgets his reading book, Ivette who is the best
in the class at everything, Yasmin who is sick on
every school trip, Jodie who owns a crazy snake
called Slinkypants, Leon who is great at rope-
swinging, Shea who knows all about blood-sucking
slugs and Zina who makes a rather disturbing
discovery in the teacher's chair...

ISBN: 978-1-84507-377-0

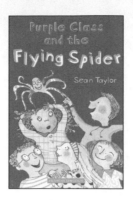

Purple Class and the Flying Spider

Sean Taylor
Illustrated by Helen Bate

Purple Class are back in four new school stories!
Leon has managed to lose 30 violins, much to
the horror of the violin teacher; Jodie thinks
she has uncovered an unexploded bomb in
the vegetable patch; Shea has allowed Bad Boy,
Purple Class's guinea pig to escape; and Ivette
has discovered a scary flying spider,
just in time for Parents' Evening!

ISBN 978-1-84507-627-6